Why
are people
Refugees?

Cath Senker

WAYLAND

Editor: Philip de Ste. Croix
Cover design: Hachette Children's Books
Inside design: Malcolm Walker
Consultant: Marion Couldrey, Co-Editor
   Forced Migration Review, Refugee Studies
   Centre, University of Oxford
Picture research: Shelley Noronha, Glass Onion
Indexer: Amanda O'Neill

Published in Great Britain in 2004 by Hodder
Wayland, an imprint of Hodder Children's Books

Reprinted in 2004

This paperback edition published in 2007 by
Wayland, an imprint of Hachette Children's Books

British Library Cataloguing in Publication Data
Senker, Cath
   Why are people refugees?
   1. Refugees - Juvenile literature
   I. Title II. De Ste. Croix, Philip
   325.2'1

ISBN 978 0 7502 5168 6
Printed by C&C Offset, China

Hachette Children's Books
338 Euston Road, London NW1 3BH

Acknowledgements
The author would like to thank the following for
their help in the preparation of this book: Ali
Brownlie; Michael Cardona; Sarah Harland and
Simba of the Zimbabwe Association for the case
study in chapter 4; Bertha Leverton for the case
study in chapter 2, from *I came alone* compiled by
Bertha Leverton and Shmuel Lowensohn (Book
Guild, 1990), Minority Rights Group for the case
studies in chapters 1 and 3; UNHCR magazine
Refugees for the case study in chapter 7.

Picture acknowledgements
The publisher would like to thank the following
for their kind permission to use their pictures:
Camera Press 31, 32; Corbis (*cover*) (Peter Turnley);
Exile Images (*contents*) (bottom) (M. Kobayashi), 4
(J. Hawkins), 15 (Howard Davies), 17 (R. Chalasani),
18 (Howard Davies), 20 (M. Kobayashi), 21 (H.
Ruiz), 22 (M. Kobayashi), 25 (Howard Davies), 27
(Howard Davies), 37 (C. Smith), 40 (Howard
Davies), 42 (Howard Davies), 43 (R. Chalasani), 44
(Howard Davies); Wayland Picture Library 12, 13
(Imperial War Museum), 36 (UNRWA); Popperfoto
(*imprint page*) (Louis Gouliamaki), 9 (Claro Cortes,
Reuters), 10, 11, 16 (Corinne Dufka, Reuters), 24
(Gregg Newton, Reuters), 26 (Howard Burditt,
Reuters), 28 (Louis Gouliamaki), 29 (Jerry Lampen,
Reuters), 30 (Claro Cortes, Reuters), 33 (Guillermo
Granja, Reuters), 35 (Tim Wimborne, Reuters), 38
(AFP), 41 (Matthew Green, Reuters); The Refugee
Council 45 (Tash Law); Rex (*contents*) (top) (Kevin
Weaver), 5 (Kevin Weaver), 6 (Kevin McKiernan,
Sipa), 8 (Sipa), 19 (Mark Peters), 23 (Sipa), 34
(Wilhelmsen), 39 (AA/Sipa); Topham Picturepoint
14.

Cover picture: Kurdish refugees in Turkey,
10th April 1991.

Contents

1. Who is a refugee?

Forced to flee

Esperanza, aged fifteen, had to escape to another part of Colombia when soldiers killed her father in 1997. Elvira, a thirteen-year-old, was forced out of her home in Kosovo in 1999 and brought to safety in Britain. Felipe, a 22-year-old Mexican, had been homeless and unemployed since leaving school. He entered the USA illegally in 2001 and found work as caretaker of an office block.

▲ *These children have been forced to leave their homes and move to another part of Colombia in South America because of civil war. They are being cared for by a charity.*

Which of the above are refugees? According to the 1951 United Nations Convention, a refugee is someone who has fled from his or her country and cannot return 'owing to a well-founded fear of being persecuted for reasons of race, religion, nationality, membership of a particular social group or political opinion.' Refugees who have been persecuted and claim the right to asylum – a safe haven in the country they've arrived in – are known as asylum seekers.

▲ *These Kosovans had to flee their homes in 1999 after Serb forces took over their land. Most went to nearby countries and some were accepted by western European nations.*

Esperanza did not leave her country. This makes her an Internally Displaced Person. Felipe was not persecuted but he lived in poverty, so he moved to another country to work. He is classed as an 'economic migrant'. According to the UN definition, the only genuine refugee is Elvira.

This book will look at the many reasons why people are forced to leave their homes, whether because of conflict, fear of persecution or desperate poverty.

FACT:
Some 21 million people were internally displaced by the end of the 1990s, compared to 13-14 million in 1990. About 12 million people in the world are legally accepted as refugees. Between 75 and 80 per cent of the approximately 50 million refugees and displaced persons around the world are women and children.

UNHCR

Refugees, IDPs and economic migrants

◀ *Mexican farm workers in the USA. Migrants typically work as agricultural labourers, building workers or cleaners. They tend to do the jobs that local people prefer not to do.*

So what exactly are the differences between these three groups? Refugees and internally displaced persons (IDPs) have been forced to leave home for the same reasons. Usually they live in an area of conflict and are in danger. The difference between IDPs and refugees is that refugees have left their own countries and crossed an international border to another country. IDPs move to another part of their own country. The great majority of refugees move to other poor countries. Most people in both groups come from the poorest countries of the world.

FACT:
One person out of every 115 people alive today is a refugee or displaced person. There are refugees living in every country in the world but most of them have been taken in by the poorer countries of Africa and Asia. Most of the world's internally displaced people also live in these countries.
Refugee Council, 2002

The issue of economic migrants is a complicated one. People have always moved from country to country to seek work and better opportunities. You might know people who have moved to another country to work. Perhaps they have moved from or to the UK, Europe, Australia, the USA or Canada.

Yet many of the poor people who migrate to richer countries to work do not move simply for a better standard of living. For example, Kurds have moved in large numbers from Turkey to Germany to work. Jobs are much better paid there. But life is also difficult and dangerous for Kurds in Turkey, where they are not allowed to speak their own language or practise their culture. So persecution is another reason for leaving. Many do not come as refugees, but you can see that the difference between economic migrants and refugees isn't always clear.

weblinks

For more information about internally displaced persons, go to www.waylinks.co.uk/ series/why/refugee

▼ *A map showing the numbers of refugees living in each major region of the world on 31 December 1999. The greatest numbers are in the poorest regions of the world.*

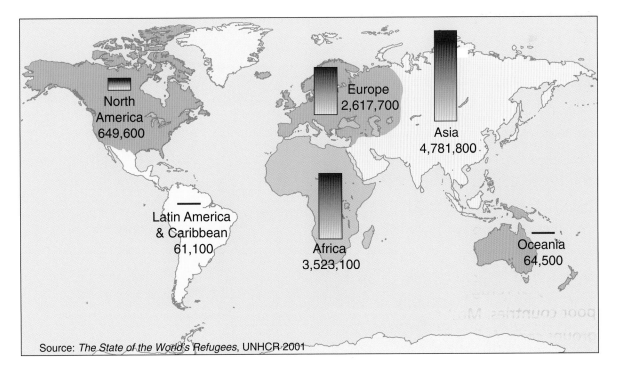

North America 649,600

Europe 2,617,700

Asia 4,781,800

Latin America & Caribbean 61,100

Africa 3,523,100

Oceania 64,500

Source: *The State of the World's Refugees*, UNHCR 2001

Child refugees

Imagine having to pack up a few precious things and say goodbye to your home and family, perhaps for ever. Over half of the world's refugees are children. Half of them are in Africa, of whom two million live in Sudan. Children might have to flee on their own because their parents have been killed or they have been separated from them. Maybe the parents have sent them away because it is their only chance of survival.

Unaccompanied child refugees and IDPs suffer from particular difficulties. Without anyone to look after them, they are at greater risk from disease and hunger. Adults or older children may abuse them. Some armies recruit refugee children because they are cheap to feed and easy to influence. Sometimes they are forced to become soldiers as the only way to get food.

weblinks

For more information about refugee children, go to www.waylinks.co.uk/ series/why/refugee

◀ *Refugee children in Somalia. In refugee camps people may be short of food and have to live in dirty conditions, putting children at particular risk. Older children often have to take responsibility for caring for younger brothers and sisters.*

Refugee children can suffer from terrible trauma. They may have seen horrendous violent acts. Perhaps they have seen family members being brutally murdered. Even if they are lucky enough to reach a refugee camp, there may be no teachers there to educate them. Many children spend years away from their homes, often in different places. The average amount of time a child is displaced is six years in Africa and Asia, and seven years in Latin America. And what future do children have without proper education?

▲ *Afghan refugee girls at a class near Islamabad in Pakistan in 2002. The Afghan government had not allowed girls like these to go to school.*

case study · case study · case study · case study · case study

'My name's Lul Ugas. When I was a little girl I lived in a town called Howadaag in Somalia. It was great over there. I lived with my mum, dad, brother and sister. After my father died, I lived with my mum for about a month. Then we children had to travel to Ethiopia because there was fighting in my country.

'We couldn't stay in Ethiopia because it was too expensive so we moved to Yemen. After two years there was fighting there, so we moved back to Ethiopia for six months. Then we all had to travel to England.

'I would like to live with my mum. I always think of her and I will always remember her.'

2. The history of refugees

Creating borders

People have always moved to seek work or avoid conflict. For most of human history, people only had to cross natural borders, such as seas, mountains or deserts. If they came across other people, sometimes they were welcomed. At other times, however, they fought them for the right to use the land. In some countries, rulers built walls to keep out other people. For example, the Great Wall of China was built in the third century BCE to keep out the Mongol people.

The fixing of borders began around 500 years ago when nation states began to form in Europe. European countries were growing more powerful and developed strong governments to run them. A sense of national identity grew – a belief that people who came from a country belonged there while others did not. For example, in 1601, Queen Elizabeth I made Africans leave England. It was a time of famine and unemployment and England's rulers chose to blame Africans for the problems. They were seen as different from the white majority and therefore very easy to target.

From the seventeenth century onwards, European powers started to take control of other parts of the world in a process called colonialism. They fought to seize large parts of Asia, Africa and the

'...the Queen's majesty...greatly distressed in these hard times...is highly discontented to understand the great number of Negroes and blackamoors [black Africans] which...are crept into this realm.'
Royal Proclamation, Queen Elizabeth I of England, 1601

Americas and established borders between the lands.

Often, people from different ethnic groups lived in the same land. The rulers tended to favour one group at the expense of another, causing divisions in society. For example, in nineteenth-century India, the British rulers favoured the Hindus over the Muslims. This kind of policy led to conflicts, which later caused waves of refugees.

▲ In this early twentieth-century photo, servants are waiting on their colonial masters in Bangalore, India. British rulers made local Indians work for them.

◀ Muslim refugees pouring out of India and into the new state of Pakistan after the partition of India in 1947. As soon as India was divided, Hindus and Sikhs started killing Muslims in India, and Muslims killed Hindus and Sikhs in Pakistan. It is estimated that about 12 million people switched countries to avoid the violence.

11

The Second World War and its aftermath

The Second World War caused the biggest movement of refugees the world had yet seen. When Adolf Hitler rose to power in Germany in 1933, his Nazi government took away Jewish people's rights and forced them out of most jobs. They were arrested and attacked, and their property was burnt to the ground. By 1939, half of Germany's Jewish population of 525,000 had emigrated.

Between 1939 and 1941 Hitler invaded many European countries. The Jews were trapped in Nazi-occupied lands and few managed to escape. Other countries did little to help, although individuals in Denmark, Norway and France helped Jews to flee. Six million Jews were murdered by the Nazis.

About 60 million people were forced to leave their homes amid the death and destruction caused by the Second World War. Afterwards, the United Nations set up a special organization called the United Nations Relief and Rehabilitation Administration (UNRRA) to help refugees and displaced people to return home.

▼ *In the early part of the Second World War, millions of Jews in Nazi-occupied European countries were forced to move to ghettos in Poland. They were then sent to death camps to be killed. In 1943, people in the Warsaw ghetto rose up against the Nazis but they were defeated, as this photograph shows.*

Many did not want to return, such as two million Soviet citizens who were unhappy about returning to communist rule. But they were forced to go. Many Jewish people did not want go back to countries where they had been persecuted. Some were allowed to travel to the USA and others managed to go to Palestine in the Middle East.

Modern warfare since 1945 has uprooted people in similar ways and caused huge movements of refugees.

▲ *These refugees have returned to Greece after having fled their country during the Second World War.*

case study · case study · case study · case study · case study

In November 1938, the British Government agreed to take 10,000 Jewish children from Nazi Germany. In 1939 one of them, Inge Hack from Nuremberg in Germany, then aged thirteen, remembered the experience:
'It was a very sad Hanukkah [the Jewish festival of lights]. My father had been taken away, Mummy was sad and I was waiting for my transport to England. One day we received the notice that I was to go at 1 a.m....We said a very fond goodbye, not knowing then that it was the last time we would ever see each other...

'When we went ashore in England, an omnibus was waiting for us...Soon we arrived at our camp which was called Dovercourt...We spent a lovely time there...One Sunday I received a message to go to London where I was to meet my new foster family...I packed my bag, [and] said goodbye to those left behind, to make the journey to London.'

Refugees in recent times

Following the Second World War, the international community set up a system for helping refugees. The UN Refugee Convention of 1951 provided a definition of refugees (see page 4) and listed their rights, including their right to stay in a safe country and to live, work and study freely. Since then there have been various refugee crises.

weblinks

For more information about refugees in recent times, go to www.waylinks.co.uk/series/why/refugee

After the war, the Soviet Union took over many countries in eastern Europe and communist governments were established there. Many people did not want to live under communism. In one of these countries, Hungary, there was an uprising in 1956. It was crushed and some 200,000 refugees fled for safety.

▶ *These displaced people in a refugee camp in 1945 are waiting to move to another camp. After the Second World War, there were 800,000 displaced persons living in camps in Germany and Austria.*

In the 1960s and 1970s large movements of refugees took place in Africa and Asia. In many African countries wars of independence were fought against the European rulers. One of the bloodiest conflicts was in Algeria (1954–62) and many Algerians fled the violence for Morocco and Tunisia. In Asia, the war in Bangladesh in 1971 and the huge conflicts in Cambodia, Laos and Vietnam created further waves of refugees.

The 1980s brought new wars, displacing people in north-east Africa, Asia and Central America. The largest number of refugees came from Afghanistan. Following the Soviet invasion in 1979, over six million Afghans left for Iran and Pakistan. Emergencies in the 1990s included the flight of the Kurds from northern Iraq in 1991 and the violent break-up of Yugoslavia after 1991. In Africa, the genocide in Rwanda in 1994 led to the exodus of two million Rwandans. The majority of refugees today are forced to flee because of armed conflict in their country.

▲ *This refugee from Rwanda has just arrived in Benaco camp in Tanzania, 1994.*

FACT:
While Iran takes in one refugee for every 26 Iranians and Tanzania one for every 73 Tanzanians, the figure for Britain is 1 for every 972. For the United States it is 1 for every 578. The European Union, a collection of some of the richest countries in the world, hosts less than 5 per cent of the world's refugee population.
Forced Migration Review, 2002

3. Fleeing war and natural disasters

Civil war

Modern civil warfare has a huge impact on civilian populations. Civilians may try to get out of the way of the fighting or they may be forced to move by soldiers. Civil wars in the poorest countries cause the largest numbers of refugees and internally displaced persons. These countries already have weak economies and the effects of war can bring them close to collapse. Conflicts may go on for many years, making the problems even more serious.

weblinks

For more information about the civil war in Sudan, go to www.waylinks.co.uk/series/why/refugee

▼ *Soldiers from the Sudanese People's Liberation Army, the southern rebel army in Sudan, going to battle during the civil war, 1995.*

Sudan in northern Africa has the worst case of internal displacement in the world. Since Sudan gained independence in 1956, the richer, mainly Muslim Arab, people of the North have dominated the country. They have held government power, backed by the Sudanese army.

▲ *The civil war in Sudan led to famine because people could not grow their crops. This picture shows people collecting grain dropped by a plane.*

Just before independence, black African people of the poorer South formed a rebel army to fight the North. This led to civil war, which has continued on and off ever since. About four million people have had to leave their homes and move to another part of the country.

Today the Sudanese government imprisons those people who oppose it. As a result over 350,000 people have fled as refugees. Without a long-lasting peace settlement, Sudanese people will carry on leaving their homes to escape war.

"'If there is food in the south, and the soldiers stop attacking, then we will go back, but not before.'
Atak Atong, western Sudan, who had to leave his village in the south when it was attacked by pro-government forces"

Fleeing genocide

Occasionally many thousands of people have to leave their home area or escape over borders to another land because of the fear of genocide. Genocide is the planned mass killing of an ethnic or religious group, perhaps the most vicious human action imaginable.

In 1975, a party called the Khmer Rouge, led by a man called Pol Pot, came to power in Cambodia in southeastern Asia. It wanted to turn the whole country into a communist peasant society. Everyone had to work on the land, toiling for at least ten hours a day with little food. Between one and two million people died between 1975 and 1978. They were either murdered by the Khmer Rouge or died of disease or hunger. In 1978 a new government took over. The country was on the brink of famine and more than 200,000 refugees moved to the border with Thailand.

These skulls form part of a memorial to help people remember those who were killed by the Khmer Rouge in Cambodia.

In 1994, genocide occurred in Rwanda in central Africa. The conflict was rooted in colonial history. When the Belgians ruled Rwanda, they encouraged rivalry between the Tutsi, the more powerful minority, and the Hutu, who were peasant farmers. The country gained independence in 1962 but the tensions continued.

▲ *Rwandan refugees fleeing their country in July 1994, after the genocide. It is estimated that around two million people left the country.*

After the Hutu president was assassinated in April 1994, Hutu soldiers started killing Tutsis, as well as Hutus who didn't support the ruling party. Up to one and a half million men, women and children – mostly Tutsis – were killed. About 400,000 refugees fled to Tanzania and Burundi. Then Tutsi rebel forces gained control of the country. About two million Hutus, many of whom had been involved in the genocide, fled to the Democratic Republic of Congo in fear of revenge attacks. When countries turn in on themselves in such a way there is no alternative but to escape.

> 'We looked up at the Rwandan hills. The entire African landscape was awash with people, all headed our way.'
> *Maureen Connelly, aid worker in Tanzania, April 1994*

Country under attack

If your country is invaded or bombed, the chances are that you'll try to reach a safe area or attempt to leave the country altogether.

Sierra Leone in west Africa suffered a decade of violence in the 1990s. In 1991, forces from neighbouring Liberia called the Revolutionary United Front (RUF) invaded the country. The fighting uprooted more than a million people over the following three years.

By 1994, the RUF had weakened but violence against civilians continued. There was more fighting in 1997 and 1998. By the end of 1998, more than one million Sierra Leoneans remained uprooted. About 400,000 of them became refugees in nearby countries. 1999 saw a peace agreement signed but there was still some fighting and abuses of human rights.

▼ *This Afghan girl fled Afghanistan after the US attacks in 2001. She is living in a refugee camp in Peshawar, Pakistan.*

There have now been so many refugee crises that sometimes countries refuse to allow in refugees.

case study · case study · case study · case study · case study

'I'm Zacharia Wurie and I come from Sierra Leone. My school days were the best period of my life…At break time we went cycling, or played football, or we told each other stories while sitting in the sun…

'I thought that I could become a lawyer. But when I was in the fourth form, some rebels came over the border from Liberia and started a war. They said they wanted to liberate the people, but that was not true. They killed people… They burned the rich people's houses and stole everything…Sometimes the soldiers did these things too. I saw the people who had been killed on the streets by the rebels. Because of the situation I had to escape to the Netherlands in 1991.'

War has plagued Afghanistan in southern Asia since 1979 and many refugees have fled from their homes. Today 1.4 million Afghan refugees live in Iran and 1.2 million in Pakistan. Another 300,000 Afghan people are displaced in their own country.

▼ *With the cold winter approaching, Afghan refugees living in this camp in Peshawar, Pakistan had only tents to protect them.*

In 2001 the USA led a bombing campaign against Afghanistan. The aim was to root out the group that had organized the terrorist attacks in the USA on 11 September 2001. Pakistan and Iran – and the other four surrounding countries – had so many Afghan refugees already that this time they quickly closed their borders to new arrivals.

Natural disasters

A vicious cycle of war and natural disasters can cause huge movements of people. In sub-Saharan Africa there is often not enough water for crops, animals and people. A drought results. During wartime, such problems become worse. People may not be able to tend their crops properly. The crops are then more likely to fail, leading to famine.

People usually show great strength and are very resourceful, making the best of difficult circumstances. Yet war makes coping with drought or famine even more difficult. It is hard to travel to find food and water. Food prices rise. Often fighting armies will seize what food there is, leaving civilian populations hungry.

During the late 1970s and early 1980s in north-east Africa, war and famine led to mass movements of people. In 1984, a famine developed in Ethiopia. The world's television screens filled with horrifying pictures of starving people holding their weak, hungry children. There was a mass exodus of around 300,000 people to Sudan; others went to Somalia and Djibouti. It is thought that one million Ethiopians died.

▼ *These Ethiopian refugees fled to Somalia in 1980 to avoid fighting in their country. The famine in 1984 led to a further exodus from Ethiopia.*

It was generally believed that drought and poor harvest caused the famine. Yet another central problem was war. Forces in Eritrea and Tigray, which were ruled by the Ethiopian government, were fighting for independence from Ethiopia. As part of the military campaign between 1980 and 1985, the Ethiopian army seized food supplies and rationed food for civilians. During the famine, Ethiopia would not allow international relief organizations to help people in areas controlled by the Eritrean and Tigrayan forces. This made the suffering even greater.

▲ *Food aid from the European Community arriving in Ethiopia during the famine, 1984.*

FACT:
Environmental projects can cause the mass displacement of people. In 2001, the Turkish government was planning to build the Ilisu Dam in south-east Turkey. The dam was to be built as part of a hydro-electric project to provide electrical power. It was going to affect 78,000 people, mostly Kurds. As many as 25,000 would have lost their homes, land and livelihood. Their land and villages would have been flooded by the huge reservoir created by the dam. In 2002 the project was halted because of a large international campaign which put pressure on the construction companies involved and persuaded them to stop work.

4. Abuses of human rights

Abuse and persecution

This chapter looks mostly at refugees according to the 1951 UN definition – people who are fleeing persecution. A very important reason why people become refugees is because their human rights are not respected in their own country. Maybe they are fighting for an independent state within the country. Perhaps they oppose the government, but this is forbidden in their country.

Other refugees may be from ethnic minorities who suffer from racism. They may follow a religion that is not accepted in their country. They decide to leave to escape persecution. When human rights are seriously abused, the numbers of people fleeing the country increases.

▶ *A member of the Tingui Boto people taking part in a peaceful protest outside the Justice Ministry in Brazil, 2002. Members of several indigenous peoples in Brazil were concerned about a new law that they believed was harmful to their interests.*

 *Maya refugees from Guatemala in El Porvenir refugee camp in Mexico, 1990. They left their country to escape violence. During the 1980s there was a civil war in Guatemala over land and human rights. At least 20,000 Maya were killed by the army.*

In Colombia in South America there is a fierce struggle between the government and opposition forces, which has been particularly violent since 1992. During 2001, the army and its paramilitary allies, and also opposition groups, continued to commit grave human rights abuses. Civilians were the principal victims.

The statistics are chilling: in that year over 300 people 'disappeared' (usually taken away by the army never to return, presumably killed). More than 4,000 civilians were killed – mostly by paramilitary groups backed by the army. Large numbers of people were displaced and more than 1,700 people were kidnapped, mainly by guerrilla groups. It is no wonder that people caught up in such conflicts try to escape.

> 'The paramilitaries were pressuring me to collaborate with them: "Work with us or leave the area or die." But to join up with them means working against our neighbours. That's why we had to leave.'
>
> *Displaced peasant farmer in Barrancabermeja, Colombia, who left his home in 1995*

Opposing the government

In certain countries it is illegal to oppose the government or join a trade union. Even so, some brave people may still be active in organizing unions or demonstrations, or producing anti-government newspapers. These courageous acts may at some point mean they are likely to be thrown into prison. They may even receive death threats. So they make the agonizing decision to leave.

A state of terror exists in Zimbabwe in Southern Africa. Robert Mugabe was elected president in 1980. Since about 1985, he has tried to prevent opposition and to increase his own power.

▲ *Riot police in Zimbabwe controlling crowds of voters during the 2002 elections. President Mugabe managed to crush the opposition and remain in power.*

case study · case study · case study · case study · case study

'I'm Simba from Zimbabwe. Six weeks after the elections in 2000, my wife and I were attacked by the police for being MDC supporters. I was held in prison for weeks and was tortured so badly that I lost track of time. After being dumped in the bush I eventually returned home. My family scraped together the money for a plane ticket to the UK.

'A fortnight after I arrived, I found out that my wife had died because of the injuries she received during the attack. I applied for asylum in the UK and was sent to Wandsworth prison for six months. I had to stay in my cell for 23 hours a day. In the end I was refused asylum.'

In 1999, a new political party, the Movement for Democratic Change (MDC), was formed. It proved very successful. When the MDC gained nearly half of the seats in the 2000 election, Mugabe sent the army and police to punish its voters. The following year he brought in a law stating that anyone caught criticizing him was to be sent to prison. Since 2000, many Zimbabweans who oppose Mugabe have fled abroad.

Myanmar (a country in southeastern Asia which used to be known as Burma) is another country that does not allow political opposition. In 1990, the National League for Democracy, led by Aung San Suu Kyi, won 82 per cent of the seats in the parliamentary election. But the military government ignored the vote and put dozens of elected NLD leaders in prison, including Aung San Suu Kyi. Anyone who is suspected of opposition risks imprisonment, torture and execution. In December 1999, there were 127,800 refugees living outside Myanmar.

▶ *Aung San Suu Kyi talking to activists fighting for democracy in 1996. In 2000 she was placed under house arrest (she could not leave her home) and was not released for nearly two years.*

Ethnic cleansing

Sometimes people are forced to leave their country because they belong to an ethnic group that the rulers will no longer tolerate. Former Yugoslavia was made up of six different nations: Serbia, Croatia, Slovenia, Montenegro, Bosnia and Albania. Within each nation lived different ethnic groups. When the government collapsed in 1991, war broke out between these ethnic groups. The most powerful group, the Serbs, conquered large parts of the country. Some of the worst fighting was in Bosnia and about 700,000 Bosnians fled.

The Serb leader, Slobodan Milosevic, wanted to remove all non-Serbs from the areas he conquered. Throwing out people from a different ethnic group became known as 'ethnic cleansing'. Many were driven out of their homes, put in prison, tortured and executed. In the town of Srebenica, in Bosnia in 1995, Serb forces killed 7,000 Bosnian Muslim men and boys in the worst atrocity in Europe since the Second World War.

A region called Kosovo was taken over by the Serbs. Further conflict erupted in 1998 between Serb forces and the majority group in Kosovo, who were ethnic Albanians – people of Albanian origin.

▼ *This Albanian child is one of many who fled from their homes in Pristina, Kosovo in 1999 after Serb forces took control of the region. The refugees are resting in a village just over the border in Macedonia.*

About 850,000 ethnic Albanians fled for their lives, mostly to neighbouring countries. Some went to other European countries, including the UK.

> 'We had to help. We are ethnic Albanians and these people needed us. We cooked together and slept on the floor...But it was no problem. There really wasn't anything else to do.'
>
> *Rexhep Murseli, Macedonia, 2001*

For instance, in March 1999, Serb forces invaded the village of Zhegra in Kosovo. Fourteen civilians were killed before ethnic Albanian Mitant Zimani, her husband and children managed to escape to the hills. They began a 30-hour trek to safety in neighbouring Macedonia. Across the border, Rexhep Murseli and her nine children – also ethnic Albanians – took them in.

In 2001, Slobodan Milosevic was put on trial as a war criminal for the death and destruction caused by ethnic cleansing.

▼ *Slobodan Milosevic (seated) at his trial for war crimes in the Hague, the Netherlands, 2001. The Serb leader was accused of being responsible for the murder of hundreds of ethnic Albanians, and for forcing out about 800,000.*

5.Leaving for a better life

The rich-poor divide

weblinks

For more information about Somali refugees in Kenya, go to www.waylinks.co.uk/ series/why/refugee

The yawning gap between rich and poor countries has been getting wider since the mid-1970s. Now, it seems that the process of globalization is making it even larger. Giant transnational companies want to be able to produce goods and run services wherever they like, usually at the lowest cost. They believe this will bring down the price of goods, create jobs and allow wealth to trickle down through society. Yet small producers, such as peasant farmers, cannot survive in competition with these big companies.

For example, the Mexican government used to help farmers to buy seeds and fertilizers. In the 1980s they stopped this aid. Mexican farmers could not compete with the huge farms in the USA and Canada. Many of them gave up their farms to become migrant farm workers living in the USA.

▶ *An Afghan shoe seller at work in Pakistan. Afghanistan is one of the poorest countries in the world and this man left the country to find more profitable work.*

The growing rich–poor divide causes many people worldwide to migrate to make a living. They are called 'economic migrants'. They are not seen as being in fear of persecution and are not classed as refugees.

▲ Migrant workers harvesting green peppers in California, USA. The majority of migrant farm workers in the USA are immigrants.

Some Somali refugees who have fled their war-torn country, Somalia, are now living in camps in Dadaab, Kenya in east Africa. They are not allowed to work outside the camps and it is hard to set up businesses inside them. Many refugees rely on money sent to them by family members working in other countries to survive.

It could be argued that there isn't a great difference between people with a genuine fear of persecution (refugees) and those who are forced to migrate abroad to make money so their families do not starve – economic migrants.

FACT
An average factory worker in the USA earns about four times as much as a Mexican factory worker and 30 times as much as a Mexican agricultural worker.
New York Times, 18 July 2000

Economic crisis

Polish factory workers earn about £150 a month. Some go to Germany in their summer holidays to pick asparagus, where they can earn about £500 a month. After communism collapsed in the Soviet Union and eastern Europe in the early 1990s, many people found that their incomes dropped and they lost the benefits of a government welfare system. Thousands began to come to western Europe to find work.

However, in 1992, a single European community was created in western Europe. It became the European Union in 1993. People from within the community were allowed to move freely between member countries to live and work. It became harder and harder for people from other lands, including eastern Europe, to migrate legally to the European Union.

Kurdish refugees arriving in Italy by boat, 2002. Despite the dangers, some Kurdish refugees will pay vast sums of money to people who can smuggle them into Italy. They are desperate to escape persecution and poverty.

People in Ecuador queuing outside the Spanish embassy in the capital, Quito. They want to apply for a visa that will allow them to work in Spain. In Ecuador, around 70 per cent of the people cannot afford the basic things they need to live.

In many developed countries, migrant workers cannot enter freely. Yet it is accepted that they will come, often illegally, to take on the dirty, low-paid jobs such as farm work, which locals don't want to do.

Cubans fleeing Fidel Castro's communist regime for the USA after 1959 used to be welcomed with open arms. They were accepted as political refugees, who preferred the American way of life to communism. In the early 1990s, the Soviet Union broke up and could no longer give support to its communist ally, Cuba. As poverty increased in their country, greater numbers of Cubans left for the USA. In 1994, with thousands arriving, the US government decided they would no longer be accepted, but would be placed in detention camps if they came.

FACT
There are a large number of illegal eastern European migrants working in the UK. Wages for unskilled work are as low as £100-£160 a month. A worker earning the legal minimum wage would earn about £660 a month for a 35-hour week (before paying tax).

The debate about migration

The USA is a wealthy country, built by people from all around the world. The biggest groups are whites, African-Americans, Asians, Hispanics (people from Latin American countries living in the USA) and Native Americans. Historically, the USA has welcomed refugees and is a 'melting pot' of different cultures. Europe is a wealthy region. Its population has been falling as fewer children are born, so more workers are needed to keep the economies going. So why are refugees and immigrants rarely welcomed nowadays?

In the 1960s unemployment grew in Europe and the USA. There were no longer enough jobs for everyone. Since then, immigrants have often been blamed for the problem. The argument was that if there were no immigrants, there would be enough jobs for local people. Politicians took up the cry and introduced immigration controls. This call to keep out foreigners has now extended to asylum seekers, who are seeking refuge from persecution.

▶ *A boat from the Norwegian ship,* Tampa, *which rescued nearly 300 Afghan refugees from their sinking craft in the Indian Ocean in 2001. The refugees were trying to get to Australia but Australia would not accept them.*

weblinks▶

For more information about immigration in the USA, go to www.waylinks.co.uk/series/why/refugee

A demonstration in support of asylum seekers outside a detention centre in Sydney, Australia in 2002. Inside, asylum seekers had been on a hunger strike – refusing to eat. They were protesting at the length of time it took for their applications for asylum to be dealt with.

In many European countries and also in Australia, people who want to claim asylum are locked up in detention centres as soon as they arrive. They are treated with suspicion, commonly seen as criminals trying to cheat their way into the country rather than people with a genuine fear of persecution. They have to prove that they really are escaping from a murderous regime before they are allowed to stay.

> 'An increase in workers usually expands the economy and so increases the jobs available for native workers…That is why a million Cubans lifted the economy of Miami out of slump, and a million French colonists returning from Algeria [1962] lifted the south of France.'
>
> *Nigel Harris, Professor of Urban Economics, University College London, 2000*

In the media, refugees are often referred to as 'swamping' the country with a huge 'wave' of foreigners. People are led to believe that their numbers are far higher than they actually are. They may become concerned that their country cannot afford to support the newcomers, and this can lead to bad feelings towards refugees and even racism.

35

6.Without a homeland

Longing for their land

People only leave their country as refugees if there is no other alternative. They want to return home as quickly as possible. But sometimes they do not have a homeland to go to. Maybe it has been taken over by other people and they are no longer welcome there.

weblinks

For more information about the lives of young Palestine refugees, go to www.waylinks.co.uk/ series/why/refugee

In 1948, the State of Israel was formed. It was a country for Jewish people, who did not previously have a homeland. That year, during a war between the new state and the surrounding Arab countries, Israel took 78 per cent of the land. Out of about 1.3 million Palestinian Arabs, nearly one million were driven from their homes and land. Most escaped to areas called the West Bank and Gaza Strip or to nearby Arab countries. The majority found shelter in refugee camps. During a later war in 1967, Israel conquered the West Bank and Gaza Strip too. Following that war many Jewish refugees were welcomed in Israel.

▶ *A Palestinian family living in Jabaliya refugee camp in the Gaza Strip. Because of curfews, the children cannot go to school and have to study at home.*

▲ *Palestinian women protesting in 2001, because Israeli soldiers have taken over a house in the West Bank to use as a base for their operations, forcing them from their homes.*

More than 50 years after Israel was founded, most refugees in the West Bank and Gaza Strip still live in tiny makeshift homes in refugee camps, with no running water. At the end of 2001, more than half of Palestinians in the West Bank and Gaza Strip could not afford to buy the basic things they needed to live. The Palestinians have fought two uprisings against Israeli rule and have murdered Israeli citizens. The Israelis have responded by destroying their homes, stopping them from travelling freely and killing hundreds of people. The Palestinians hope that eventually they will win their own state where they can live in freedom.

> 'In 1948, our village near Nazareth was attacked by the Israeli army. I was six at the time. We fled to Ain al-Hilweh in Lebanon. My ten-year-old brother got lost in the rush and we've never seen him since. I don't suppose we'll ever be able to return. But I've still got the key to our old house.'
>
> *Joumana, Palestinian refugee living in Lebanon*

Fighting for freedom

Struggles between the government and groups that are fighting for their own independent state can lead to massive internal displacement and refugee movements. For instance, over 20 million Kurdish people live in Iraq, Turkey, Iran, Syria and Armenia. The Kurds are an ethnic minority in all these countries, with their own culture and way of life. They have no nation of their own but are struggling for an independent homeland, Kurdistan. In Iraq the Kurds were persecuted by Saddam Hussein's armed forces.

After Iraq was defeated by the USA and its allies in the Gulf War of 1991, the Kurds rebelled. Iraqi forces then attacked them. About 1.3 million fled to Iran. Another 450,000 trekked through the mountains to the border with Turkey. But Turkey would not let them in. A 'safe haven' for the Kurds was established in northern Iraq. The 2003 war in Iraq brought an end to Saddam Hussein's rule, but the Kurds in Iraq still face an uncertain future.

weblinks

For more information about Kurdish refugees who fled Iraq, go to www.waylinks.co.uk/ series/why/refugee

◀ *Kurdish refugees fleeing Iraq in 1991. They had joined the unsuccessful rebellion against the Iraqi dictator, Saddam Hussein. He then took revenge on the rebels.*

In Turkey, the Kurds are not even recognized as a people. They are forbidden to speak their language or practise their culture. Kurdish books, poetry and holidays are all illegal. During the 1990s, the Kurdistan Workers Party (PKK) led an uprising against Turkish rule. The Turkish army destroyed thousands of Kurdish villages, displacing the inhabitants, in an attempt to stop people supporting the PKK. Torture and killing of Kurds became common. The PKK ceased to exist in 2002 but the persecution of Kurds continues.

A few thousand Kurds managed to escape and seek asylum in Europe. Until they can live freely and safely in Turkey and Iraq, there will be further movements of refugees and displaced people.

▲ Turkish forces enter the Kurdish region of northern Iraq, preparing to attack Kurdish guerrilla fighters from the PKK, 1995. During the 1990s, the Turkish army often entered the region, which was outside Iraq's control, to fight the PKK.

FACT
Around 3,000 Kurdish teachers, trade unionists and other professionals have been killed by death squads in Turkey.
KurdishMedia.com 2002

7. Going home

Choosing to go home

Most refugees have strong memories of their homeland throughout their years in exile. What they want above all is for the conflict there to end so that they can go home. When this happens, it is called voluntary repatriation. (Repatriation means going back to your country.)

Refugees are often so keen to go back that they return even if the situation is still not entirely safe. They may have no homes or land to go back to, and there may be no basic facilities such as water or electricity supplies. Yet they return anyway. In June 1999 a peace plan for Kosovo (see pages 28-9) was agreed. Within three weeks, 500,000 Kosovan Albanians had returned. By the end of 1999, more than 820,000 had gone back. It was the quickest return of refugees in history.

weblinks

For more information about refugees going home to Kosovo, go to www.waylinks.co.uk/series/why/refugee

▼ *These Kosovan Albanian children returned to their homes in Kosovo in 1999 to find that they had been destroyed by Serb forces. The Albanians made huge efforts to rebuild their homes, hospitals, schools and roads.*

After Ethiopia took over Eritrea in east Africa in 1962, there was a bitter 30-year civil war. From 1967 onwards, about 500,000 people were forced to flee to neighbouring Sudan, another poor country. Around a quarter settled in refugee camps. In 1993 Eritrea achieved independence but then there was another war between Ethiopia and Eritrea, which finished in 2000. Finally in 2001 the refugees started to return from Sudan.

▶ *Eritrean refugees shaking hands with friends as the train leaves to take them back home, after 30 long years in refugee camps in Sudan.*

case study · case study · case study · case study · case study

'My name is Kidane Maasho. I fled Eritrea with my wife two decades ago after our village was bombed by Ethiopian warplanes. Thirteen of our neighbours were murdered by soldiers. We escaped through the desert pushing our herd of 20 cattle, donkeys and goats. In Sudan, we had to sell our herd to survive and then we had to move into a refugee camp. There was no work and nothing to do. But we made friends and raised seven children there.

'Now we have returned to Eritrea. I have been waiting for this day for 20 years. Sudan has been very good to me and my family. I thank my God for keeping me long enough to see this day. I am old and weak, but I have finally made it home.'

Forced to go home

Sometimes refugees are forced to return home against their will. Most refugees are 'pushed' to go home. The host states – the countries where they are living – stop helping them. Or they are 'pulled' by promises of land or improved human rights if they go home – promises which may not be fulfilled. If they have lived in exile for many years, they may have settled, raised families and become part of a new community. Forcing them to go back means uprooting them once more.

Some refugees may have nowhere to go back to. Their home and community may have been destroyed. If there has been 'ethnic cleansing' they may no longer be welcome in the area.

◀ *Rohingya refugees queuing for water in Dumdumia camp on the Bangladesh-Myanmar border in 1992. The Rohingya were forced to go back to Myanmar even though it was not safe for them to do so.*

In 1991–2, a quarter of a million Muslim refugees, known as the Rohingya, fled from Buddhist Myanmar (Burma) to Muslim Bangladesh to escape serious human rights abuses (see page 26–7). They lived in refugee camps there. But Bangladesh is very poor. At first the refugees were helped. But from late 1992, tens of thousands were forced to go back. They were told their food rations would be cut and were threatened with violence if they didn't. The Rohingya returned to continuing human rights abuses in Myanmar and some had to flee once more.

After the genocide in Rwanda in 1994, about 580,000 people fled to neighbouring Tanzania. In December 1996, the Tanzanian government and the United Nations High Commissioner for Refugees stated that all refugees could return to Rwanda in safety. Refugee leaders did not agree. The Tanzanian government used troops to force the refugees across the border into Rwanda.

> 'It was like trying to load the ark two-by-two, but the waters had already reached shoulder level.'
>
> *Aid official trying to control the flow of Rwandan refugees returning from Zaire in 1996*

▼ These Rwandan refugees were forced by Tanzanian soldiers at gunpoint to return to Rwanda in late 1996. Here they are crossing Rusomo bridge on the Rwandan border.

The future

While there are conflicts, human rights abuses and natural disasters, there will always be people forced to flee and become refugees. During the twentieth century, warfare came to mean all-out war against civilian populations, hugely increasing the numbers displaced by conflict. Global warming means that floods and other environmental problems are likely to become worse. They will cause further movements of population.

▲ A demonstration against the bad treatment of asylum seekers in London, 2001. The slogan 'hands off my friend' was the name of the campaign. It was supported by trade unions, some MPs, student groups, celebrities and many ordinary people.

For those refugees who manage to escape to another country, the difficulties are mounting. The poor countries that receive the majority of refugees suffer from a lack of resources. In richer countries, new harsh rules make it harder for refugees to enter and gain permission to stay.

We should realize that refugees can make an important contribution to the countries where they live. Some refugees have become world famous, such as Albert Einstein, a Jewish scientist who fled the Nazis in 1933. Duc Tran was a refugee from Vietnam who built a huge business empire importing popular Asian fruits to the USA.

Refugees bring a wealth of skills, talents and culture and play a valuable role in their new country. Maybe you are a refugee yourself or have refugees at your school. Many of the people you know will have parents, grandparents or great-grandparents who were refugees.

Is there a solution to the issue of refugees? Closing the huge rich–poor divide between and within countries would certainly help to reduce conflict in the world and the need to escape from it. In the meantime, many organizations are helping refugees, campaigning to improve their rights and informing the public about why they have fled. As individuals we can join them to extend a warm welcome to those escaping persecution and terror in their own land.

> 'Elis is a great player and he's really friendly. He's just like anyone. He's just like us.'
> *Kevin McArron, 14, about his team-mate Elis Suferi, a 13-year-old asylum seeker from Macedonia who scored a hat-trick, taking his school into the Glasgow schools soccer final*

▼ *The victorious Somali team in the National Football Festival, a competition for London's refugee communities.*

GLOSSARY

Abuses, human rights
Not allowing people their human rights (see below) and treating them badly.

Assassinated
A famous or important person killed for a political reason.

Asylum seekers
Refugees who claim the right to live in safety in another country because they have been persecuted in their own land.

BCE
Before the Common Era – before the birth of Jesus, when the Christian calendar starts.

Civil war
A war between groups of people in the same country.

Civilian
A person who is not in the armed forces or the police force.

Colonialism
When one country rules over another land as if it owned it.

Communism
The system of government in the former Soviet Union and a few countries, such as Cuba, today. Under communism, the government, not individual people, controls the production of goods and running of services.

Convention
An official agreement between countries or leaders.

Detention camp or centre
A place where refugees are held while it is decided whether they are allowed to stay in the country.

Drought
A long period of time when little or no rain falls.

Economic migrant
A term that is used for people who move to another country to make a better living.

Emigrated
Left to live permanently in another country.

Ethnic group
A group of people who share a common culture, tradition and sometimes language.

Ethnic minority
A group of people who have a different culture, religion, language or skin colour from most other people in their society.

Exodus
When many people leave a place at the same time.

Famine
A lack of food in a region over a long period of time.

Genocide
The deliberate killing of everyone of a particular ethnic group.

Global warming
The increase in temperature of the Earth's atmosphere. It means there will be more floods and other environmental problems.

Globalization
The free operation of businesses all around the world, investing where they want, trading in whatever goods and services they want and employing labour wherever they want.

Guerrilla group
A band of fighters that make war against a regular army.

Homeland
The country where a person was born. Some people, such as the Kurds and the Palestinians, do not control their own homeland.

Human rights
Rights to basic human needs such as a home, food, work, health care and education. Also included are political rights, such as the right to vote. The United Nations Convention on Human Rights states that countries have to respect these rights.

Immigrant
A person who comes to live permanently in another country.

Immigration controls
Controls to limit the number of immigrants that can come into a country from certain other countries.

Internally Displaced Person (IDP)
A person who has been forced to leave the area where he or she lived and move to a different part of the same country.

Migrant
Someone who moves from one country or region to another.

Military government
A government controlled by the armed forces.

Nation state
An independent country formed by people who share the same culture and language.

Paramilitaries
Military groups that help the official army of a country.

Persecuted
Treated badly, often because of the person's ethnic group, culture, religious or political beliefs.

Ration
Limit the amount of food people are allowed to have.

Refugee
A person who has been forced to leave their country, usually because of war or persecution.

Relief organizations
Organizations, such as the Red Cross and Oxfam, that help out in an emergency.

Transnational companies
Companies that operate in many countries.

United Nations
An association of many countries that aims to improve social conditions and to solve political problems in a peaceful way by consultation and negotiation.

Welfare
Practical help, such as money or services, given to needy people.

FURTHER INFORMATION

ORGANIZATIONS

United Kingdom
Amnesty International
The Human Rights Action Centre
17-25 New Inn Yard
London
EC2 3EA
Tel: 020 7033 1500

Minority Rights Group
International
54 Commercial Street
London E1 6LT
Tel: 020 7422 4200

Refugee Council
240-250 Ferndale Road
Brixton
London
SW9 8BB
Tel: 020 7346 6700

Refugee Studies Centre
Queen Elizabeth House
21 St Giles'
Oxford
OX1 3LA
Tel: 01865 270722

Australia
Refugee Council of Australia
Suite 4A6, 410 Elizabeth Street
Surry Hills
NSW 2010
Tel: 03 9416 0044

North America
American Red Cross National
Headquarters
2025 E Street, NW
Washington
DC 20006
Tel: 202 303 4498

Amnesty International USA
5 Penn Plaza
New York, NY 10001
Tel: 212 627 1451

Canadian Council for Refugees
6839 Drolet #302
Montréal
Québec H2S 2T1
Canada
Tel: 514 277 7223

National Network for Immigrant
and Refugee Rights
310 8th Street
Suite 303
Oakland
CA 94607
USA
Tel: 510 465 1984

US Committee for Refugees
1717 Massachusetts Avenue, N.W.
2nd Floor
Washington DC
20036
USA
Tel: 202 347 3507

International
United Nations
High Commissioner
for Refugees (UNHCR)
1211 Geneva 10
Switzerland

BOOKS TO READ

Just the Facts: Refugees by Steven Maddocks (Heinemann, 2004)
In the News: Immigration and Assylum by Iris Teichmann (Oxfam Educational, 2002)
One Day We Had To Run by Sybella Wilkes (Evans, 2000)
Refugee by Angela Neustatter (Franklin Watts, 2005)

WEBSITES

For websites that are relevant to this book, go to www.waylinks.co.uk/series/why/refugee

INDEX